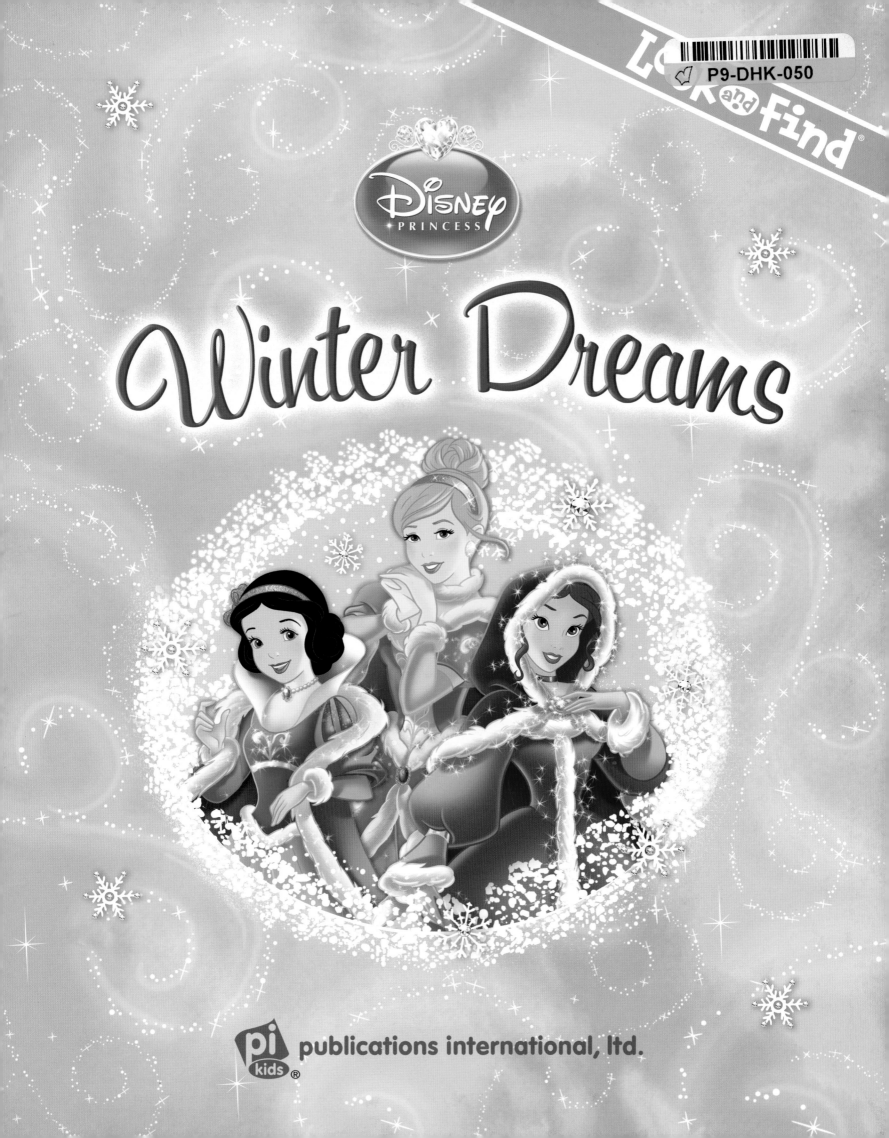

Disney PRINCESS

Winter Dreams

pi kids®

publications international, ltd.

The Beast loves Belle and wants to make all her wishes and dreams come true. As they stroll around the snow-covered grounds, see if you can find the ice sculptures that remind him of Belle:

swan

rose

Phillipe

hearts

mirror

books

Rapunzel has been dreaming up all kinds of gift ideas to help her stay busy through the winter. See if you can find these projects she is working on:

house for Pascal

paper angels

candle

colorful quilt

gingerbread house

snowman ornament

Princess Aurora and Prince Phillip are enjoying a dreamy winter sleigh ride in their beloved glade. As they head off to visit the good fairies, look for these white animals hiding in the snow:

mouse

this rabbit

this snowy owl

cat

dove

fox

wolf

The weather might be cold and blustery, but it's warm and cozy inside the gift shop! As Ariel dreams up special ways to surprise her family and friends, look around the shop and see if you can spot these gifts for people on her list:

pocket watch

dog dish

shell-shaped ornament

ship in a bottle

nautical pendant

music box

Snow White's wish has come true! All her friends are ice skating on a wonderful wintry day. As they slip, slide, or glide around the frozen pond, look for these forest friends who have joined in the fun:

clowning chipmunk

whirling bird

bouncing bunny

galloping goose

twirling squirrel

rambunctious raccoon

ice-dancing deer

Jasmine has set her sights on visiting a pretty mountain village on a moonlit winter night. As she and Aladdin prepare for their landing, look around and find these colorful houses:

Ever since she was a little girl, Tiana dreamed of owning a restaurant. Now that Tiana's Palace is open, she couldn't be happier. Look around and find these delicacies she is preparing to celebrate festival season in New Orleans:

bread pudding

king cake

beignets

praline pie

fruitcake

fleur-de-lis tart

With a wave of her magic wand, the Fairy Godmother granted Cinderella's wish to put on the perfect winter party for all her friends. Look around the beautiful ballroom and see if you can find these festive decorations:

candelabra

this wreath

silver bell

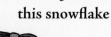

this snowflake

mistletoe

poinsettia

punch bowl

Belle and the Beast
are sharing a heartwarming
moment in the garden. Circle around
the castle grounds to find these icy
likenesses of the enchanted objects:

Coatrack

Cogsworth

Lumiere

Featherduster

Mrs. Potts

Footstool

Chip

There's been a flurry
of activity in Rapunzel's
tower during the winter months.
Head back and find these tools she
needs for her projects:

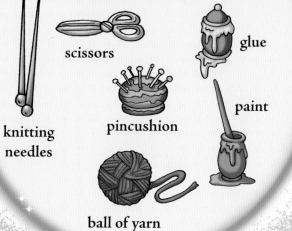

scissors

glue

paint

pincushion

knitting
needles

ball of yarn

Aurora has always
counted on the Good Fairies to
help make all her dreams come true.
Head back to the glade and
count the following things:

sprigs of winter berries (16)

pinecones (13)

sleigh bells (9)

red birds (8)

icicles (7)

snowmen (3)

After getting presents
for everyone on her list, Ariel
decides to treat herself to a beautiful
snow globe. Visit the gift shop
and find some she might like:

Twirl back to Snow
White's ice-skating party to see
if you can find these things lost
in the hustle and bustle:

mittens

cape

stocking cap

scarf

muff

earmuffs

Jasmine and Aladdin
are well matched in every way.
Fly back to the mountain village
and find six pairs of lacy snowflakes
that are perfectly matched too:

With a splash of this
and a dash of that, Tiana has been
busy baking many delicious treats.
Revisit her kitchen and find
these key ingredients:

cinnamon

butter

powdered sugar

eggs

milk

flour

Go back to the ballroom
and see if you can find these
dazzling tiaras on Cinderella's
well-dressed guests:

ruby tiara

diamond tiara

emerald tiara

sapphire tiara

silver tiara

gold tiara